The
FRIENDSHIP
FACTORY

The FRIENDSHIP FACTORY

William L. Coleman

BETHANY HOUSE PUBLISHERS
MINNEAPOLIS, MINNESOTA 55438
A Division of Bethany Fellowship, Inc.

Photos by Dick Easterday

Published by Bethany House Publishers
A Division of Bethany Fellowship, Inc.
6820 Auto Club Road, Minneapolis, Minnesota 55438

Printed in the United States of America

Library of Congress Cataloging-in-Publication Data

Coleman, William L.
    The friendship factory.

    Summary: Devotions in verse, accompanied by Bible verses, explore the many aspects of sustaining good relationships with others.
    1. Children—Prayer-books and devotions—English
[1. Prayer books and devotions. 2. Conduct of life.
3. Christian life] I. Title.
BV4870.C6319   1986   242'.62   86-17137
ISBN 0-87123-670-2 (pbk.)

Mary Coleman did an excellent job of helping
to prepare this book.

Also in This Series

About the Author

BILL COLEMAN has written several bestselling devotional books for this age group (three to seven) besides his very popular family devotional books for older children and teens. His experience as a pastor, a father and a writer help to give him his special relationship with children. He and his family make their home in Aurora, Nebraska.

Contents

For Caring Parents and Teachers,

Each of us would like to see children behave well, treating others with kindness, thoughtfulness and consideration. This book is designed to help guide children into good relationships. Rather than take a chance that they might get along well with others, these chapters are aimed at promoting solid, wholesome behavior.

As you spend time reading, I hope God gives you a special bond with the children in your life. May they learn respect for their friends and live happily with others.

Bill Coleman
Aurora, Nebraska

Helping Out

Today is a good day
To do something for
Somebody else.

Today is a good day
To take a few minutes
And plan
What you could do
For others.

People do plenty
Of things for us.
They bake,
They sew,
They clean,
They build,
They share,
Because they want
To be nice to us.

Today is a good day
To do something for
Somebody else.

"Each of you should look not only to your own interests, but also to the interests of others." (Phil. 2:4)

A Chatter-Box

Mrs. Elmwood used to tell
Her daughter, Peggy,
"Don't be such a chatter-box."

That meant Peggy talked
All the time or chattered
And didn't take time
To listen.

Many of us get that way
Sometimes.
If the teacher begins
To tell us how to do
Something
And we keep talking,
We act like a
Chatter-box.

Smart people learn
To listen.

If we talk all
The time,
We won't know what
Is going to happen
Next.

If we talk all
The time,
We won't know where
We are going
Next.

If we talk all
The time,
We won't know when
We are supposed to
Leave.

Smart people learn
To listen.

Sometimes we need
To talk.
Sometimes we like
To talk.
Sometimes we can
Hardly wait
To talk.

But we can't talk
All the time.

Smart people learn
To listen.

"Jesus called the crowd to him and said, 'Listen and understand.' " (Matt. 15:10)

Being Neat

It's all right for
Babies to be
Sloppy.
They haven't learned
Any better.

When a baby
Finishes eating,
There is often a mess
All around the table
And on the floor.

When a baby
Gets hold of
A newspaper,
He tears up
The paper and
Even tries to
Eat it.

That's why we
Keep newspapers
Away from babies.

As we grow up
We learn to be
Neat.

We pick up
Our clothes.
We put things
Where they belong.

And we
Place things back
On the table
If we knock them off.

It's more fun
To be around
People who are
Neat.

It's safer to walk
In their room
Because we don't
Trip on things.

And it's easier to sit
On their chairs
Because we
Won't sit on anything.

Babies can be sloppy,
But children
Should know how
To be
Neat.

"But everything should be done in a fitting and orderly way." (1 Cor. 14:40)

Why People Like You

People like you
Because
Of the way
You act.

You aren't pushy.
You don't like
To fight.
You don't scream
When you don't
Get your way.

People like you
Because
Of the way
You talk.

You are careful
What you call
People
And the words
You use.

People like you
Because
You like people
And you are
Kind to them.

You have friends
Because
You act like a

Friend
And you are
Nice to people.

"Even a child is known by his actions, by whether his conduct is pure and right." (Prov. 20:11)

The Number One Friend

We might have friends
Of all sizes and
All ages.

Friends who live
Far away and
Friends who live
Close by.

Friends we see
Every day and
Friends we have
Never met.

Some of us have
Ten or twenty friends
While others have
One or two
Special friends.

No matter who
Our friends are,
There is one
Special Friend
That each of us
Should have.

His name is
Jesus Christ.

This friend is special
Because He is
The Son of God.

This Special Friend
Forgives us when
We have sinned.

He walks with us
Every day
To school,
To the playground,
Or anywhere.

This Special Friend
Has made a place
In heaven where
We can live
Forever.

If we ask
Jesus Christ
To become
Our Special Friend,
He will become
A special
Part of our lives.

"I have called you friends." (John 15:15)

When You're Sorry

Every once in a while
We hurt someone's
Feelings.

We say something bad
About their clothes
Or make fun of
Their hair.

Maybe we broke
Their toy
Or threw
Their candy
In the mud.

We have hurt their feelings
And we would like
To make them
Feel better.

When we tell them
We are sorry and
We mean it,
We usually make
Them feel better.

Some people hate
To say
They are sorry.
They would rather
Stay away
From their friend.

Running away
Makes everyone feel
Worse.

Saying we are sorry
Is good for friends.
It draws them closer
And keeps them friends
For a long time.

Good friends
Tell each other
Words that
Make them
Feel great.

**"I am sorry for what I have done."
(Ps. 38:18, TLB)**

Including Others

Angie really liked people.
She met as many children
As she could,
And played with them
Whenever she had time.

She never thought
About
Whether they were poor
Or rich.
She never thought about
Whether they were fast
Or slow.
She never thought about
Their skin color or
Where they were born.

She invited all kinds
Of friends
To her backyard.

And she never said
Nasty things
About others.

Angie tried hard
To do what Jesus
Told her to do.
In the Bible
Jesus told her
To love others
The same way
He loved her.

Angie liked that.
Loving people seemed
Like the best thing
To do.

Angie opened her yard
To all kinds
Of people
Because Angie
Really liked people.

"Love one another. As I have loved you, so you must love one another." (John 13:34)

Picking on People

Have you ever watched
Two people
Begin to pick on
Another person?

They make fun of
The way he
Plays ball or
The way he
Sings or
The kind of books
He carries.

We call this
"Picking on people."

If you have ever
Been picked on
By other people,
You know how
Miserable that
Can be.

Most of us
Pick on others
Sometimes
Even though
We know
It is wrong.
And we know
It hurts.

All of us
Like to be
Treated with
Kindness.
God wants us
To carefully
Treat others
With kindness, too.

It's no fun
To have people
Pick on us.
It's no fun
To pick
On others,
Either.

That's why we
Are kind
To others.

"Always try to be kind to each other and to everyone else." (1 Thess. 5:15)

Changing Faces

Let's pretend
Your job today is
To change people's faces.

It isn't as hard
As it sounds.
You can change
Most people's faces
In less than
A minute.

And all it will
Cost you is
A few words.

When you see
Your friend,
Tell him how
Much you like
His bike
And watch his face
Change into a smile.

Or tell him
He is a *good* friend,
And watch his face
Change into a smile.

All of us need someone
To say something nice
To us.
Kind words make
You and
Others feel better.

Be a face changer
Today.
With just a few words
You can paint a smile
On your friend's face.

"How good is a timely word!" (Prov. 15:23)

Watch a Hippo Eat

Have you ever been to the zoo
And watched a hippopotamus chew
Its food?

Have you seen peanuts and lettuce
Bouncing around inside the hippo's
Large mouth?

And have you thought to yourself,
"I wish he would close his mouth
When he eats"?

When you see someone eat
With his mouth open,
You see something ugly.

Food hopping around,
A tongue jumping
Up and down.

The food inside a hippo's mouth
Looks more like garbage
Than it looks like food.

The next time you go
To the zoo,
Whisper something to
The hippo.

Tell him he would look
A lot better if
He would close his mouth
While he eats.

**"Each one should test his own actions."
(Gal. 6:4)**

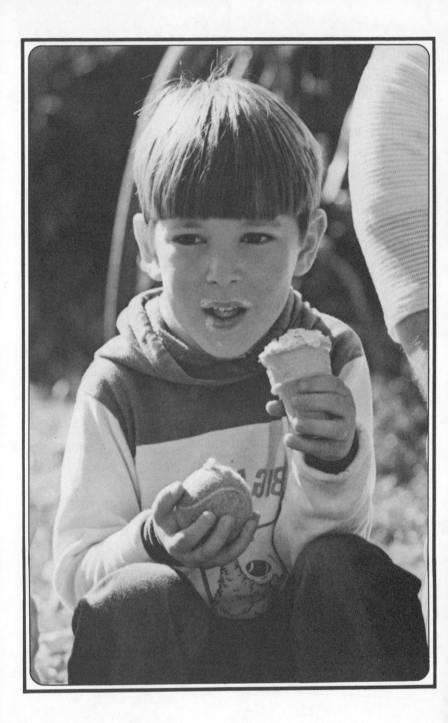

Keeping Secrets

Wendy told Robin a secret,
And she didn't want Robin
To tell anyone.

That was a hard job
For Robin because
Robin was friendly
And she liked to talk.

Robin said "Hello"
To the mailman
And she almost
Told the mailman
Wendy's secret.

Robin was playing
With Vicky and
She started to tell
Wendy's secret,
But she stopped.

Robin was drying
The dishes with
Her brother, Arnold,
And she wanted
To tell him
About Wendy's secret,
But she bit her lip
And kept it inside.

Before bedtime that night
Robin sat on the couch
Between her mother
And her father.
She felt great!

Robin had been
A good friend
Because
She didn't tell
Wendy's secret
To anyone.

"A gossip betrays a confidence, but a trustworthy man keeps a secret." (Prov. 11:13)

Feeling Better

Megan sat on the steps
With her head
In her hands.

She was terribly sad
And didn't want
To talk to anyone.

When Cindy saw Megan,
She wondered what she
Could do to make
Her friend feel better.

Cindy went home and
Picked up her big box
Of dolls.

She carried the box
Over to Megan's house
And plunked it down
In front of her friend.

Megan didn't even look up—
Not right away.
Then, slowly she let her eyes
Drift over to the box
To take a quick glance
At the dolls.

A tiny grin appeared
On Megan's cheek,
And her dimple opened
Slightly.

"Let's play together,"
Said Cindy.

Megan picked a doll
Out of the box
And smiled.
She spent the entire
Afternoon having fun
With Cindy
Instead of being sad.

Cindy knew that
Friends need friends.
So she decided
To help
The same way
God helped her
When she
Was sad.

**"So that we can comfort those in any
trouble with the comfort we ourselves have
received from God." (2 Cor. 1:4)**

Being First

We like to be first
In a race.
It feels good to win
And know we did
Our best.

But we don't have
To be first
At everything
We do.

Sometimes we enjoy
Seeing others be first.

We let others in line
First.
We let others pick
Baseball gloves
First.
We let others answer
First.

We don't need
To push
Or pull
Or shove
Or hurt
So we
Can be first.

Today we will be
First
To use the crayons.
Tomorrow Mary can be
First.

And the next day Larry
Can use the crayons
First.

Everyone gets a chance.
And being first isn't
Really important.

Sharing, caring, helping—
Those are much more
Important
Than being first.

It's great to be
Around friends
Who don't have to
Be first
All of the time.

"Honor one another above yourselves."
(Rom. 12:10)

Name Calling

We all get called names
Sometimes.
Maybe you have been called
Stupid,
Dummy,
Fatty,
Bonehead,
Or Knobby Knees.

Maybe you have been called
Other names like
Pokey,
Porky,
Shy,
Slow,
Lug head,
Chicken
Or
Basement breath.

You have probably
Felt bad
Because someone
Called you a name.
It can hurt
To be called
Names.

It's no fun
To hurt people.
That's why
We don't call people
Bad names.

Sometimes we call
A person a name
Like "Goofy"
And the person laughs.
But inside
He hurts.

It's better to call
People by their real names
And say good things
About them.

It's no fun
To hurt people.
That's why
We don't call people
Bad names.

"Reckless words pierce like a sword, but the tongue of the wise brings healing." (Prov. 12:18)

Friends Wait

When you have a friend,
You learn to sit on the steps
And wait for him.

If you have to sit
While he finds
His lunch money,
You don't mind
Because
You are good friends.

When you have a friend
You wait
In the hall
While he gets his books.

You don't yell or
Stomp off or
Get upset if
You have to wait
Once in a while.

Sometimes you wait
For him and
Sometimes he waits
For you.

People who like people
Are patient with
Each other.

"Be patient with everyone." (1 Thess. 5:14)

Happy Jokes

Happy jokes are the ones
That make you laugh
When you hear them,
And make you laugh
Later
When you remember them
Again.

Happy jokes are the ones
You can tell to anyone
And not be embarrassed,
And not have to blush,
And not be ashamed of.

They are the jokes that
Sometimes make your sides
Ache,
Or even bring tears
To your eyes because
You laugh so hard.

Happy jokes don't need
To have dirty words,
Make people feel bad
Or pick on people
Who look different
Or come from other
Countries.

Good jokes can be shared
With your parents,
With your teachers,
With your pastor,

And
With your special
Friend.

Happy jokes do not hurt.
Happy jokes are not cruel.
Happy jokes are never told
To be mean.

Good jokes are
Good for everybody.

"Nor should there be . . . foolish talk or coarse joking which are out of place." (Eph. 5:4)

How Would You Like It?

How would you like it
If your friends
Let you swing first
Or if your friends
Said nice things
About your hair
Or your clothing?

You would probably like it
And you would feel good.

How would you like it
If your friends
Invited you to their houses
And shared their toys
With you
And taught you how
To play a new game?

You would probably like it
And you would feel good.

How would you like it
If your friends
Introduced you to
More friends
And went with you
To the park
And spent time
With you?

Think of the things
You would like
Your friends to do
For you.

Make a list
In your mind
Of the things
You would enjoy.

How would you like
To be treated?
How would you like
To be spoken to?

Jesus told us
To treat others
The same way
We would like
To be treated.

If all of us
Treat others
That way,
We will be
Good friends,
Getting along well.

**"Do to others as you would have them do
to you." (Luke 6:31)**

First in Line

When Mrs. Andrews said
The ice cream bars were ready,
The children ran in from
The playground.

As Tom ran past Jay
He pushed him and
Jay fell down.

Tom was the first one
In line
And he was happy to
Be there.

Slowly Jay got up,
Brushed himself off
And went to
The end of the line.

Tom wasn't a bad person,
And Tom didn't like
To hurt people,
But sometimes Tom
Forgot.

Tom forgot about
Being kind to others.
Tom forgot about
Being careful.

All Tom could think about
Were the ice cream bars
And himself.

God knows we forget.
That's why He put
A note in the Bible
To remind us
To think about others
And stay away from
Pushing.

"Love is patient, love is kind." (1 Cor. 13:4)

Keeping Promises

If we tell somebody
We will be someplace,
We keep our promise
And we get there.

If we tell a friend
He can use our tape,
We keep our promise
And we loan him
Our tape.

Friends are people who
Do what they say
They will do.

If we tell a friend
We will help him
Paint a wagon,
We keep our promise.

If we tell him
We will help
Pick up when we
Are done playing,
We keep our promise.

Friends are people who
Do what they say
They will do.

Once in a while
Something happens

And we can't keep
Our promise.

When that happens,
We try to tell
Our friend why
We can't keep it.

Promises are too important
To merely forget about.
Promises mean too much
To break them.

Friends are people who
Do what they say
They will do.

"It is far better not to say you'll do something than to say you will and then not do it." (Eccles. 5:5, TLB)

54

Everybody Likes a Compliment

How do you feel
When someone says
He likes your new bike
Or your baseball glove
Or your shirt?

It makes you feel good,
Because everyone enjoys
A compliment.

If someone says she likes
Your hair
Or the way you smile
Or the way you put
Your toys away,
It makes you feel good,
Because everyone enjoys
A compliment.

When we give compliments
To others, it makes them
Feel great, too.

We tell our friends
That we like
Their clothes or hair,
Their pet or toys,
And we make them
Feel good.

All of us like
To hear compliments—

Mothers and fathers,
Brothers and sisters,
Grandmothers and
Grandfathers,
Teachers and store clerks.

They might be having
A terrible day,
But a compliment
Will pick their head up
And put a smile on their face.

Compliments are free.
Compliments are helpful.
Compliments are happy.

Everybody enjoys a compliment.

"An anxious heart weighs a man down, but a kind word cheers him up." (Prov. 12:25)

Whispering

If we listen carefully,
Sometimes we can hear
The wind whispering.

The wind knows how
To be loud and
Powerful.

The wind can rustle
Through the trees
And make the windows
Of our house
Rattle.

But the wind can
Be gentle.

Sometimes if we stand
In our yard
And we stay completely
Quiet,
We can hear the wind
Whispering
As it moves gently
Through the leaves
And past the house.

Some days the ocean waves
Will beat against the shore,
Making a terrible
Crashing noise.

But other days they roll
Smoothly over the beaches,
Peacefully and quietly.

Often people need to
Talk quietly or
Whisper
To their friends
Just like the wind
And the waves.

Too much noise
Makes people tired,
And grouchy,
And fussy.

That's why God
Created whispering,
So we could talk
Softly
Some of the time.

"He stilled the storm to a whisper; the waves of the sea were hushed." (Ps. 107:29)

Friends We Haven't Met

In some countries
There are boys and girls
Who never get enough
To eat.

In some cities
There are boys and girls
Who don't have enough
To wear.

We have probably
Never met these people
Who live far away,
But we have heard
About their needs.

These boys and girls
Are the
Friends we haven't met.

They are still our friends
Because they have needs
And we can help them.

When we can,
We send them
Clothes and food
And money
Because we have
Much more than
They have.

We give things
To our parents
Or to our church
To be sent
To the boys and girls
We have not met.

Christians have always
Given to help
Those who are suffering,
Because people in need
Who live far away
Are the
Friends we haven't met.

"The disciples, each according to his ability, decided to provide help for the brothers living in Judea." (Acts 11:29)

The Big Friendship

You have never seen God
Because God is a Spirit.
But you can believe in God,
And that makes God
Your friend.

Every day you receive
Good things that God
Has created for you—
Like water, food,
And people who care.
They are gifts sent to you
From God.

God is probably bigger
Than we are
If we could measure
His size.
But that doesn't stop
God from being part
Of the lives of
Little people.

God is someone to talk to,
Someone to share with,
Someone to follow,
Someone who will
Always stay close by you.
God makes a great friend.

When you
Do things that
Are wrong,
God still loves you
Just like a good friend.

Some people
Don't understand
About God.
They are afraid
Of God
And want Him to
Stay as far away
As possible.

But God is love.
He wants to help
And walk through life
With everyone.

Do you believe in God?
Do you love God?
Is God your friend?

" 'Abraham believed God, and it was credited to him as righteousness,' and he was called God's friend." (James 2:23)

She Never Cheats

Tiffany is an excellent friend.
No matter what you play
With her, you know
She never cheats.

Her friends don't have to
Watch her every minute,
And don't have to
Stay in the room to
Keep an eye on her.

Tiffany doesn't cheat,
Doesn't want to cheat,
Doesn't even think of cheating.

Tiffany knows that cheating
Is wrong
And playing fair
Is good.

People like to do things
With Tiffany.
She is someone
You can always trust.

**"Love does not demand its own way."
(1 Cor. 13:5, TLB)**

Asking Permission

How do you feel
When someone takes
Something
That belongs to you?

If someone takes
Your bike
And doesn't ask
If they can use it,
You might get
Angry.

If someone takes
Your game
Without your
Permission,
You might feel
Sad.

All of us need
To remember
To ask permission
And say
Kind things like
"May I"
And "Please."

Kind and pleasant
Words
Make people feel
Good.

When we just take
Something,
Our friends may feel like
We've stolen it.

We keep our friends
Happy
And are allowed to use
More things
By using pleasant
And kind words
Like "May I"
And "Please."

"Pleasant words are a honeycomb, sweet to the soul and healing to the bones." (Prov. 16:24)

Having Your Own Way

All of us enjoy
Having our own way.

We like to play
Our favorite game.
We hope they will cook
Our favorite food.
We like to watch
Our favorite show.

It's all right to be
That way
Some of the time.
But if we always
Want our way
And never want
To do it their way,
We are acting
Selfishly.

It feels good to say
"Let's do it your way."
Good friends ask
"How would you like
To do it?"

It isn't selfish
To want things.
But it is selfish to insist
On our way
All of the time.

Kind people try to find out
What others would like.

We all like to be
With people who
Are willing to do
What others like,
Too.

**"An unfriendly man pursues selfish ends."
(Prov. 18:1)**

Tracy's Yard

Tracy's mother told her
She could play in the yard,
But she couldn't leave
The yard until
After lunch.

When Ginger came over
To play ball,
She wanted
Tracy to go across the street
To the playground.

Tracy refused to leave.

Ginger asked Tracy
To go.
Ginger begged Tracy
To go.
Ginger pleaded with Tracy
To go.
Ginger yelled.
Ginger pouted.
Ginger argued.
Ginger stomped.
And Ginger nagged.

Tracy looked at the house
And wondered what her mother
Would do if she left.

Tracy looked at Ginger
And listened to her plead.

Finally, Tracy gave in
And went to the playground.

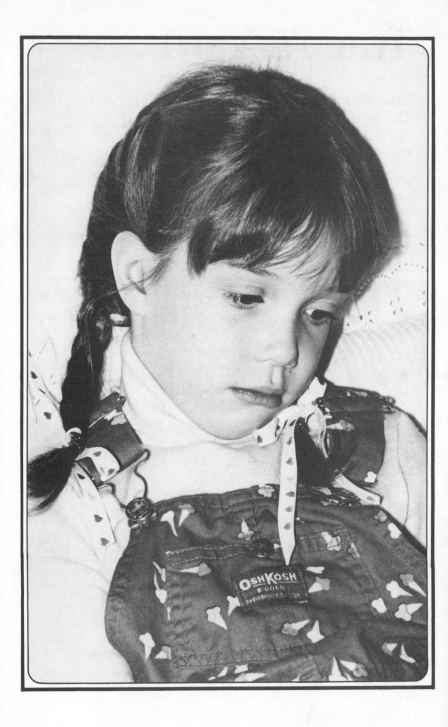

When Tracy returned home
For lunch,
Her mother was very upset.

And Mother told Tracy
She had to stay inside
All afternoon and all evening.

Tracy went to her room.
She wished
Ginger had not nagged her.

Tracy wished she
Would have
Listened to her
Mother.

God wants
Children to
Listen to and
Obey their parents.

"Whoever gives heed to instruction prospers." (Prov. 16:20)

Not a Complainer

Have you ever been
Around people who
Complain all the time?

They don't like anything.
The soup is too hot.
The milk is too warm.
The chair is too large.
The window is too high.
They never seem to be
Happy.

People who complain
All of the time
Aren't much fun
To be around.

They don't like anything.
The marshmallows are too hard.
The store is too far.
The box is too heavy.
And the food is "icky."

People who complain
All of the time
Aren't much fun
To be around.

Even God must get tired
Of people who

Complain to Him
And are never thankful
For anything.

None of us want
To be so grumpy
That we complain
All of the time.

Let's be careful
To be thankful
For the good things
We have.

People who complain
All of the time
Aren't much fun
To be around.

"Do everything without complaining."
(Phil. 2:14)

Good Losers

Mr. Peterson hated to lose.
If he was playing checkers
And he was losing,
He would cheat when
The other player left the room.

All during the game
Mr. Peterson would argue
And quarrel and complain
About the way the game
Was being played.

If Mr. Peterson lost
The game of checkers,
He would get angry
And say the game
Wasn't played fair.

Then he would walk
Outside
And stand in the yard
And refuse
To talk to anyone.

If someone played checkers
With Mr. Peterson once,
They usually didn't like
To play with him
A second time.

Some adults can't stand
To lose.
They often argue
And get upset.

Then people don't want
To play with them.

Maybe when they
Were children
They never learned
To be good losers.

We are foolish
To argue
And quarrel
Over games.

Friends are important.
Games aren't important.

**"But every fool is quick to quarrel."
(Prov. 20:3)**

Throwing Fits

Have you ever seen
Chimpanzees
At the zoo
When they begin
Throwing things?

They jump around
And scream
And begin tossing
Food.

Some zoos have to
Put glass walls
Between the animals
And the people
So the visitors
Won't get hit
With flying food.

A chimpanzee
Looks just like
A young person
Throwing a fit.

Some children
Get upset
And start jumping
Up and down.

They often yell
Or even throw things.

And sometimes things
Get broken because
They refuse to control
Themselves.

They are acting like
Monkeys.

Aren't you glad
You can control
Yourself?

You can talk
In a calm voice
And explain things
In a proper way.

You don't have to
Throw a fit.

"A fool gives full vent to his anger, but a wise man keeps himself under control." (Prov. 29:11)

Pets Are Friends

Do you have a pet
Who means something special
To you?

Maybe it is a dog with
Big ears and a cold nose.
Maybe it is a cat with
Gray fur and green eyes.

Certain animals
Make good friends.
We get to know them
And what they are like
And how they act.

They play with us
In the yard and
Chase things like
Balls, sticks and string.

Pets let you know
How much they like you
By rubbing against your leg
Or purring or climbing up
On your lap.

Boys and girls show
How much they like
Their pets by the way
They take care of them.

They feed their pets
And give them fresh water
And teach them good habits.

Good friends never hurt
Their pets
Or fail to take care
Of them.

We can thank God
For pets
Because they make such
Good friends.

"A righteous man cares for the needs of his animal." (Prov. 12:10)

Quick to Forgive

When Lisa dropped
Mary's music box,
The top broke off.

Mary was mad.
She got angry
And yelled at Lisa.

But Mary was angry
For only a minute.
She knew Lisa
Didn't mean to drop
The music box.

"It's all right,"
Said Mary.
"I'll ask my Dad
To fix it."

Mary smiled at Lisa
As they picked up the box.

Mary could have
Stayed angry,
But she remembered
When her mother
Forgave her,
When her teacher
Forgave her,
And when God
Forgave her.

She knew how good
It felt to be
Forgiven.

So Mary forgave
Lisa, too.

Some people seem
To like to stay
Angry,
But they don't look
Very happy.

We know God
Is quick to forgive us
And we enjoy
Being quick to forgive
Others, too.

"Forgive as the Lord forgave you."
(Col. 3:13)

The Honest Way

It would be easy
To lie to our friends.
It would be easy
To trick our friends.
It would be easy
To cheat our friends.

But our friends trust us
And expect us
To tell them the truth.

It would be easy
To lie to our friends,
But we know
The honest way is
The best way.

Honesty is the best way
To keep friends.
Honesty is the best way
To show friends
That we care about them.
Honesty is the best way
To prove what
Good friends we are.

Friends believe our stories,
Friends loan us toys,
Friends have us over
To their homes,
Because they believe
We are honest.
And we are.

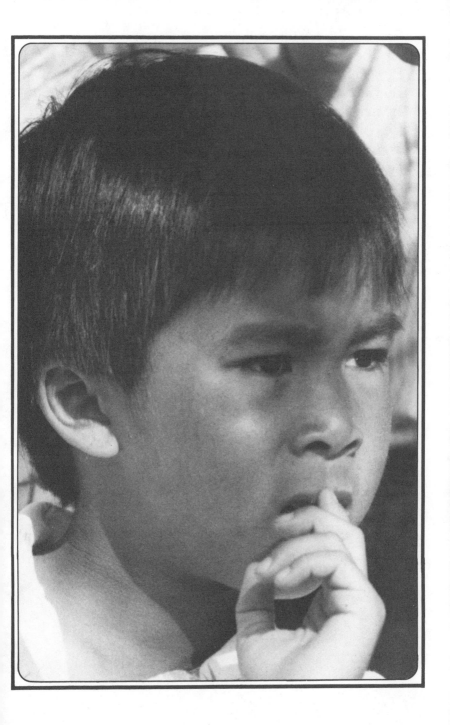

People who tell the truth
Can be trusted
By parents,
By teachers,
By neighbors,
By police,
By friends,
Because they are honest.

"Kings take pleasure in honest lips; they value a man who speaks the truth." (Prov. 16:13)

Talking Back

When your parents say
You should be home
Before dark,
You don't stomp around
And slam doors.

You know it's important
To obey your parents.

When your parents tell
You not to go
To your friend's house
Today,
You don't sit and pout
At the lunch table.

You know it's important
To obey your parents.

You might not agree
With your parents.
You might ask them
To change their minds.
You might discuss
It with them.
But you don't act
Nasty
Or talk back
Or behave like
A brat.

You know it's important
To obey your parents.

Maybe you won't understand
Why they told you
To stay home or
Be back early.
But you still won't act
Ugly.

Sometimes parents make
Mistakes.
Sometimes parents change
Their minds.
The next time they
Will try to do better.

But each time
And every time
It is better
To obey
Your parents.

"Children, obey your parents." (Col. 3:20)

Choosing Friends

A friend who
Keeps getting you
Into trouble
Is not a friend.

A friend who
Treats you badly
And does not help you
Is not a friend.

A friend who
Lies to you
And steals from you
Is not a friend.

Wise people
Are careful how
They choose friends.

Friends try to
Help friends
And not
Hurt them.

Wise people
Are careful how
They choose friends.

"A righteous man is cautious in friendship." (Prov. 12:26)

Bouncing Popsicles

When Sandy came out
The back door,
She was carrying
A plate of Popsicles.

The plate was stacked high
With red Popsicles,
And orange Popsicles,
And yellow Popsicles,
And green Popsicles.

Sandy's mother had gotten
The Popsicles for
Sandy's birthday party.
Sandy's friends
Came to play games.

When Andy saw
The heaping plate
Of Popsicles,
He took four leaps
Toward Sandy
And grabbed
A red one.

When Andy
Hit the plate,
It jumped out of
Sandy's hand
And Popsicles
Went flying
Through the air.

When they hit
The ground,
Red Popsicles,
Orange Popsicles,
Yellow Popsicles,
And green Popsicles
Bounced around
On the grass.

Andy hung his head
As he held
His Popsicle.
The other
Children
Stared at their
Popsicles
Spread out
On the ground.

"A greedy man brings trouble."
(Prov. 15:27)

When We Are Wrong

Aaron knew better than
To throw stones near
The window.
But Aaron did it
Anyway.
One of the stones
Broke a window.

When Aaron's mother asked
Him about it,
He lied and said he didn't
Break the window.

When Aaron's father asked
Him about it,
He lied and said he didn't
Break the window.

When Tommy came over
To play,
He asked Aaron about it
And Aaron lied again.

It was hard for Aaron
To admit
When he was wrong, so
He lied
And made the problem
Worse.

Most of us have
A hard time
Admitting when
We are wrong.

However, it's better
To say
We were wrong
Right away
Before we make things
Worse.

"If we confess our sins, he is faithful and just and will forgive us." (1 John 1:9)

Volcano Top

Do you have any friends
Who are volcano tops?

A volcano sits calmly
For a long time
And then suddenly begins
To blow up.

Its top blows off
And a terrible exploding noise
Is heard for miles around.

Rocks are thrown through
The air,
And hot lava starts
To pour
Down the mountain.

When the volcano begins
To blow up,
Everyone backs away quickly
So they won't get hurt.

Some of us have friends
Who are volcano tops.
Every once in a while
They start to get mad
And then
They blow up.

It's no fun to be
Around people who
Blow up
When they get upset.

Because you are
A good friend,
You control your temper.

People like you more
Because you don't have
A volcano top.

"Do not make friends with a hot-tempered man, do not associate with one easily angered." (Prov. 22:24)

The Interrupter

How do you feel
When you are trying
To talk
And someone else
Keeps breaking in?

You begin to tell
A story,
But someone interrupts
To tell his story.

You want to ask
A question,
But another person
Asks his question
Before you are finished.

All of us interrupt
Others
Once in a while
Because we forget
To be polite.

But some people
Talk all the time,
Even when others
Are trying to talk.

How often have you said,
"Does anybody know . . ."
And someone interrupted?
Have you ever said,
"Last summer on vacation . . ."
And someone else started
Telling his story?

It's rude.
It's pushy.
It's impolite
To interrupt
Others.

Have you ever
Heard a teacher
Start to ask a question
And someone interrupted
And gave the wrong answer?

That's embarrassing.

Wise people take turns
Talking
Because they like to be
Kind
To each other.

It's rude.
It's pushy.
It's impolite
To interrupt
Others.

"He who answers before listening—that is his folly and his shame." (Prov. 18:13)

The Purple Pickles

Pretend you see
A large jar of
Purple pickles
Sitting on the table
Across from you.

And you wonder
What purple pickles
Taste like.

You can feel
Your mouth watering,
And your stomach
Growling.

You can hardly
Wait to taste a
Purple pickle.

What are you
Going to do?

Reach across the table
And take the
Purple pickles?

Or yell at the
Top of your voice,
"Give me those
Purple pickles!"

You could do that,
But you know
It wouldn't be right.

If you ask for
The purple pickles
In a gentle voice,
In a kind voice,
With a happy smile,
You are more likely
To get the
Purple pickles.

"Please pass the
Purple pickles,"
Sounds just about
Right.

"Please"
Sounds friendly.
"Please"
Sounds nice.
"Please"
Sounds gentle.

We all like to hear
Gentle words like
"Please."

"Be completely humble and gentle."
(Eph. 4:2)

Laughing Together

Have you ever sat
Under a tree
In the backyard
With someone else
And laughed until
Your sides ached?

Have you ever laughed
With someone else
While you were drinking
Milk
And had the milk
Spray out of your mouth?

Have you ever laughed
With someone else
And rolled on the grass
Unable to control
Yourself?

Have you ever sat
In a room
Where you weren't supposed
To laugh,
And the two of you
Had to bite your lips
To stop from laughing
Out loud?

Have you ever sat
On a bus
And started to laugh

Because you remembered
What the two of you
Did together,
And people began
Staring at you?

God created laughter
And it was very good.

"A time to laugh." (Eccles. 3:4)

Too Much Teasing

All of us get teased
Sometimes.
And we all enjoy it
Sometimes.
But too much teasing
Can hurt.

It's no fun to have
Someone pick on us
All the time.

It's no fun to have
Someone making fun
Of the way we look,
Or the way we talk,
Or the way we run,
Or what we wear.

We might try to laugh,
But inside we feel badly.
And sometimes we even
Want to cry.

It's all right to kid
Once in a while.
It's all right to joke,
But not too often.

Good friends are careful
About feelings.

They try not to say
Words that hurt.
They are not reckless
With the words they use.

Joking and kidding are fun
As long as one friend
Does not hurt another friend.

Brothers and sisters should never
Tease too much.
Good friends should never
Tease too much
Either.

"Reckless words pierce like a sword, but the tongue of the wise brings healing." (Prov. 12:18)

When to Shout

It's all right to shout
When you're on the playground,
But you wouldn't shout
Inside your house.

It's all right to shout
When you're on the beach,
But you wouldn't shout
Inside your school.

It's all right to shout
When you are in the woods,
But you wouldn't shout
Inside your church.

Shouting can be fun,
If you know when
And where
To shout.

You wouldn't shout when
Others are reading
Or sleeping or talking.
You wouldn't shout if
It bothered other people.

If you were talking
To friends,
You wouldn't shout
At them,
But you would
Talk to them
Calmly.

Sometimes when you're feeling
Great
And you are far from
Others,
You might want to
Look up
And with all your might
Shout,
"Thank you, God,
For all you've done
For me!"

"Shout with joy to God." (Ps. 66:1)

Why Argue?

If you say it's brown,
He says it's tan.
If you say it's blue,
He says it's purple.

He likes to argue.

If you say the glass
Is half full,
He says it's about
Half empty.

He likes to argue.

If you say it's sunny,
He says it's cloudy.
If you say it's windy,
He says "Not really."

He likes to argue.

After so much arguing
You don't like to talk
To him,
Because anything you say
Merely starts an argument.

Good friends try to
Stay away from arguments.
They like to get along.
They like to be pleasant.
They like to agree
Whenever they can.

If they don't agree
They say so,
But they don't like
To argue and argue
And argue.

Good friends are careful
To disagree over important
Things,
Not to argue over dumb
Things.

"Don't have anything to do with foolish and stupid arguments." (2 Tim. 2:23)

The Happy Giver

It makes us happy
To make other people
Happy.

Some people are always
Thinking about others.
They try to do
Good things for them.

They get out a plate
Of cookies
Or bring out a box
Of toys
When their friends
Come to visit.

When they play
A game,

112

They let their friend
Go first.
And if they play
Outside,
They let their
Friend have the
First ride on their bike.

And when there is
A tray of donuts,
They give their friend
The biggest one
With chocolate on top
And cream inside.

People who give
Make the best friends
Because they don't
Have to have
Their own way.

They enjoy seeing
A smile on
Their friend's face.

That is the way
God likes to give
To us,
And that's how
We give to others.

It makes us happy
To make other people
Happy.

**"For God loves a cheerful giver."
(2 Cor. 9:7)**

Showing Off

"Watch me! Watch me!"
Kim repeated as she pulled
Bobbi's arm.

"Watch me! Watch me!"
Kim wouldn't give up
As she dragged Bobbi
Along.

Bobbi was tired of it.
It seemed like Kim
And Bobbi didn't play
Together very much.
Most of the time
Bobbi had to watch
Kim show off.

"Watch me swing."
"Watch me throw."
"Watch me build."
That's what Bobbi heard
Almost every day,
And she was tired of it.

It was fun to take turns
Doing things.
It was fun to do things
Together.
But Bobbi didn't like
Watching Kim show off
All the time.

Good friends think about
Each other

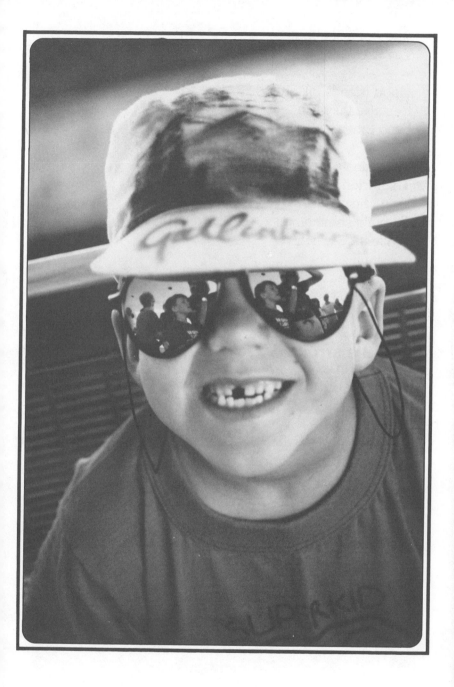

And not just about
Themselves.

Good friends take turns
Because they like
Each other.

Many times they even ask
Their friend
To go first or
To build something
While they watch.

Good friends don't have
To show off
All the time.

**"To the arrogant I say, 'Boast no more.' "
(Ps. 75:4)**

Playing Quietly

Do you have
A special friend
Whom you can
Play with
For a long time
And not say
Very much?

The two of you
Enjoy being together,
And sometimes you
Like to talk.
But other times
You like to
Play quietly.

We don't have to
Always talk or
Always make noise.

We don't have to
Bang things or
Shout at each other
To have fun.

We like to have
Our friend close
And share things,
But
We don't have to
Talk all the time.

**"A time to be silent and a time to speak."
(Eccles. 3:7)**

Giving It Back

Matthew borrowed
Jason's toy car.
When he was
Done playing with it,
Matthew put the car
On the shelf
In his own bedroom.

It was a neat car
With white wheels
And a shiny black
Body.

Matthew knew the car
Wasn't his
And he would
Give it back
To Jason
If
Jason asked for it.

But for now
Matthew would
Just keep
The car.

When Jason
Asked Matthew
About the car,
Matthew said
He would look
For it.
But Matthew still
Didn't give it back.

Jason never loaned
Anything to Matthew
Again
Because Jason liked
To get his things
Back
From his friends.

People who borrow
Have to be careful
To give things back.

"The wicked borrow and do not repay."
(Ps. 37:21)

Breaking Things

There was a boy named
Bernie the Breaker.
That wasn't his real name,
But that was what
All of his friends called him.

If Bernie's toy robot
Didn't work, he would
Throw it down and
Walk away.

If Bernie lost,
He would knock the game
On the ground.

Bernie would get upset easily.
And when he got upset,
He would do the strangest things.

Bernie the Breaker got angry
About things that didn't really matter,
Like games and toys.

And when Bernie got angry,
He did foolish things
Like throwing and wrecking
And walking away.

One day Bernie's mother
Sat down and talked
To her son
About what he was doing.

Bernie knew he threw
Things, but
He didn't know how
Bad it had gotten.

From then on Bernie tried
To behave better
When things didn't go right.

And Bernie was a lot more
Fun to be with.

**"A quick-tempered man does foolish
things." (Prov. 14:17)**

Having Our Way

All of us like
To have our way.
We like to play
Our favorite game,
Listen to the music
We enjoy the most,
Or go to the places
We pick out.

Sometimes when we
Can't have our way,
We decide to pout.

Pouting is how
We try to get others
To do what
We want.

Pouting means
We get quiet
And change our
Face
So everyone will know
We are unhappy.

Usually pouting means
We stick out our lip.
Sometimes we stick
Out our bottom lip.
Some people
Push their upper lip
Out over their
Bottom one.

We then add to
Our pouting look
By bringing our
Eyebrows down
So we will look
Extremely serious.

If we do it
Correctly,
Everyone will know
We are unhappy
Because we didn't
Get our way.

Pouting makes us
Look terrible.
Pouting makes our
Friends uncomfortable
And we are no fun
To be around.

Good friends don't
Have to always
Have their way.
Good friends can do
What others like
To do
And not pout
About it.

"He lay on his bed sulking and refused to eat." (1 Kings 21:4)

The Old Red Truck

Mark's old red truck
Has back wheels that wobble
When he pushes it
Across the floor.

It's a strong metal truck
But some of its red paint
Has been rubbed off.

When Mark's friend, Nathan,
Comes over to play,
Mark gets his new
Green truck out
And gives it to Nathan.

Nathan really enjoys
The new truck.
It has a light on top
And a small horn
On the side.

Nathan squeezes
The horn and rolls
The new truck across
The floor.
And Nathan looks
Happy.

Mark plays with his
Old red truck
With the back wheels
That wobble.

Mark and Nathan
Have good times together
Because they are friends.

After Nathan goes home,
Mark puts his old
Red truck away
And plays
With the new green truck.

Mark squeezes the horn
And rolls it across the floor,
And Mark is happy.

It feels good to share
His new truck with Nathan.
Because Nathan is his friend.

"If you come with us, we will share with you whatever good things the Lord gives us." (Num. 10:32)

Saying "Thank You"

Have you ever watched someone
Give candy bars to children?

Some children act shy and
Look at the ground when
They take their candy bars.

Other children are quick
And almost grab the candy.

If you look carefully,
You will see someone
Take the candy bar
And say, "Thank you."

The words "Thank you"
Make people feel good.

Mothers like to hear
"Thank you."
Fathers like to hear
"Thank you."
Teachers like to hear
"Thank you."
Children like to hear
"Thank you."
And
God likes to hear
"Thank you."

"Thank you" means
You like what
The person just did.

You like it when
Someone helps you.
You like it when
Someone gives you presents.
You like it when
Someone gives you clothes
Or toys
Or lifts you up
So you can see
The parade.

People are nice
And we like to
Thank them.

God is nice,
Also.
So we like to
Thank Him,
Too.

"Thank you,
God."

**"Give thanks to the Lord, for he is good."
(1 Chron. 16:34)**